FIGHTING GAMES

BY ASHLEY GISH

Apex is distributed by North Star Editions:
sales@northstareditions.com | 888-417-0195

Produced for Apex by Red Line Editorial.

Photographs ©: iStockphoto, cover; Shutterstock Images, 1, 4–5, 6–7, 7 (top), 7 (bottom), 8–9, 10–11, 12–13, 14, 15, 16–17, 18, 19, 20–21, 22–23, 24–25, 26–27, 29

Library of Congress Control Number: 2022920694

ISBN
978-1-63738-572-2 (hardcover)
978-1-63738-626-2 (paperback)
978-1-63738-728-3 (ebook pdf)
978-1-63738-680-4 (hosted ebook)

Printed in the United States of America
Mankato, MN
082023

NOTE TO PARENTS AND EDUCATORS

Apex books are designed to build literacy skills in striving readers. Exciting, high-interest content attracts and holds readers' attention. The text is carefully leveled to allow students to achieve success quickly. Additional features, such as bolded glossary words for difficult terms, help build comprehension.

TABLE OF CONTENTS

CHAPTER 1

PREPARE YOURSELVES!

Four players join a game of *MultiVersus*. Two players are on the blue team. Two are on the red team. A voice shouts, "Prepare yourselves!" The match begins.

MultiVersus is a multiplayer fighting game.

Wonder Woman bashes Batman with her shield. He flies off the fighting **platform** and out-of-bounds. The blue team scores a match point.

In many games, players try to knock one another out of a fighting area. These games are called platform fighters.

Batman and Wonder Woman are both characters from DC Comics.

FAMILIAR FACES

MultiVersus is a crossover game. That means players can fight as characters from several games, shows, and movies. Each character has different skills.

Learning to use each character's special abilities helps players win matches.

Garnet is on Batman's team. She throws her **gauntlets** at Wonder Woman. Soon, Garnet and Batman have four match points. They win the match.

FAST FACT

In MultiVersus, perks are special abilities. They let characters run faster, hit harder, or heal teammates.

CHAPTER 2

HOW FIGHTING GAMES WORK

There are many types of fighting games. Some have players fight one-on-one. Others set teams against each other.

In *Dragon Ball FighterZ*, two players battle each other.

Each time players **square**
off is called a round. A round
may end when one player gets
knocked out. Or the team with
the most points may win.

In *Tekken*, players often do sets of three or five rounds.

FAST FACT

Some games use sets or matches. Players fight a series of rounds in a row.

Players attack **opponents** to lower their health. Some characters use weapons. But many use **martial arts**. They kick and punch. They can also block or dodge to avoid getting hurt.

Players learn the best ways to block different kinds of attacks.

To do a combo, a player must press a series of buttons on the controller.

COMBOS

Combos are a key part of many fighting games. A combo is a series of moves. Players do these moves in a row. This lets them do extra damage.

CHAPTER 3

FIGHTING GAME HISTORY

The first game focused on fighting was *Heavyweight Champ*. It came out in 1976. People went to **arcades** to play it.

Arcades often had rows of machines with different games people could play.

Players try to hit their opponent until the health bar reaches zero and the opponent is knocked out.

Soon other fighting games came out. In these games, players often punched or boxed. They tried to lower their opponent's health bar.

STREET FIGHTER

Street Fighter was a series of fighting games. At first, they were arcade games. Later, people could play them at home on **consoles**.

The *Street Fighter* games were popular in many countries around the world, including Japan.

Super Smash Bros. is made by Nintendo.

MARIO 90%

Wii Fit T

In the 1990s, games added new ways of fighting. *Super Smash Bros.* had players try to knock each other off platforms. Games began using air dashing, too. Characters could flip and move through the air.

FAST FACT

Air dashing was first used in Darkstalkers in 1994.

CHAPTER 4

FiGHTiNG GAMES TODAY

Today, people often play fighting games online. They compete against people from all over the world.

Depending on the game, friends may play with or against one another.

Some players go to **tournaments**. At these events, players fight several times. They must win to advance. At many tournaments, players who lose twice must drop out.

A BIG EVENT

EVO is one of the biggest fighting game tournaments. In 2022, more than 8,000 players signed up for it. They came from 63 different countries. They competed in several different games.

EVO is a tournament that takes place in Nevada each year.

FUJIMURA

Some tournaments focus on just one game. Others have several. For some events, any player can sign up. Others are for skilled players only. People must win other tournaments to take part.

Thousands of people gather to watch the top players at tournaments.

COMPREHENSION QUESTIONS

Write your answers on a separate piece of paper.

1. Write a few sentences describing the main ideas of Chapter 2.

2. Would you like to compete in a fighting game tournament? Why or why not?

3. In what year did the first fighting game come out?

    A. 1976

    B. 1994

    C. 2022

4. How did people play the first fighting games?

    A. at arcades

    B. on consoles

    C. in tournaments

5. What does **dodge** mean in this book?

They kick and punch. They can also block or dodge to avoid getting hurt.

    A. make sure something happens
    B. move out of the way
    C. make friends with someone

6. What does **advance** mean in this book?

At these events, players fight several times. They must win to advance.

    A. be on the same team
    B. continue playing
    C. move toward a finish line

Answer key on page 32.

GLOSSARY

arcades
Places where people can play video games by putting coins into large machines.

consoles
Devices that people use to play video games at home.

gauntlets
Big, thick gloves used for fighting or armor.

martial arts
Skills used for fighting or self-defense, such as karate or tae kwon do.

opponents
Players or characters someone is fighting against.

platform
A flat ledge that characters stand on.

square off
To face one another in a fight.

tournaments
Competitions where players try to win several games or rounds.

TO LEARN MORE

BOOKS

Nicks, Erin. *Esports Competitions*. Minneapolis: Abdo
  Publishing, 2021.

Rathburn, Betsy. *Arcade Gaming*. Minneapolis: Bellwether
  Media, 2021.

Rusick, Jessica. *Super Smash Bros*. North Mankato, MN:
  Abdo Publishing, 2022.

ONLINE RESOURCES

Visit **www.apexeditions.com** to find links and resources
related to this title.

ABOUT THE AUTHOR

Ashley Gish has authored more than 60 juvenile nonfiction
books. She earned her degree in creative writing from
Minnesota State University, Mankato. Ashley lives in
Minnesota with her husband and daughter.

INDEX

A
air dashing, 21
arcades, 16, 19

B
blocking, 14
boxing, 18

C
combos, 15
consoles, 19

D
Darkstalkers, 21

H
Heavyweight Champ, 16

M
martial arts, 14
MultiVersus, 4, 7, 9

P
platform, 6, 21

T
teams, 4, 9, 10
tournaments, 24–27

R
rounds, 12–13

S
Street Fighter, 19
Super Smash Bros., 21